SHE
CHOSE
to LOVE

SHE
CHOSE
to LOVE

Yvette Dulo

YVETTE DULO

dulo.books@gmail.com
@yvette.dulo

To all of them

*For teaching me
how to stand up
for myself*

SHE CHOSE TO LOVE

SHE CHOSE TO RESIST

Engine................................*19*

Rat race................................*23*

Molotov................................*24*

*Snakes and Ladders**................................*29*

What are you afraid of?................................*35*

SHE CHOSE TO HEAL

I admit, I am afraid................................*43*

Adaptation wounds................................*44*

How is your heart today?................................*46*

Untitled 2................................*49*

This creek is a lifespring................................*51*

Heaviest rock to lift................................*52*

Under the bridge................................*53*

Come round..................................*55*

Deck of cards..............................*56*

Life long education.......................*57*

Starfish limbs..............................*58*

Sideways *59*

Shadow of a summit.....................*60*

Spoon—shaped............................*63*

Archimedes.................................*64*

Float...*66*

Old chapter, new tale...................*68*

SHE CHOSE TO BE

Construct a place.........................*73*

Edge of the blanket.....................*75*

Summer's ascending *77*

Heart waves................................*78*

Testament...................................*79*

Neck deep...................................*81*

me *84*

Sail upwards *86*

Hands of autumn *88*

Embers *90*

Be the silence *92*

A pearl in a black sea *93*

SHE CHOSE TO LOVE

Buoyancy *97*

Towards *98*

Stargazings *100*

Cosmic avocado ☉ *102*

Prism-heart *105*

Babel *106*

Clock *107*

Human condition *108*

Flame *113*

Dewdrops..*116*

She chose to love *118*

ACKNOWLEDGEMENTS

ABOUT THE AUTHOR

SHE CHOSE TO **LOVE**

"Only when we choose our path,
we feel empowered to fight on"

We all encounter a lot of adversity in our lives. Adversity others might not grasp the full extent of. Sometimes the tides are high and things quickly turn upside down.

This is when a challenge emerges—how to find strength, stand up and experience the world whole-heartedly. How to choose hope and love, despite the irreversible, despite the people who disapprove, despite.

How do you reignite the flame and keep it burning?

I hope I can share some of my flame with you through the poems of "She chose to love". To motivate self-acceptance, inner freedom and following your own path.

This book is for you. For you to find ways to rediscover flourishing and blooming, to find empowerment and tap into the inner spring.

May these poems inspire hope and unearth love, for yourself and for the world.

Let the tale of your life unfold.

LOVE,
Yvette

SHE CHOSE
TO **RESIST**

ENGINE

The engine
spews steam
unperturbed,
undisturbed

Ominous in
its breathing,
reshaping
w *o* r *d s*

Spalling hearts,
slicing hopes

I

She refuses to follow
what the steam engine
demands

Not allowing the cylinders
to dictate her daily
rhythm

Inlet and exhaust valves
to open and close
and control
the flow of her life

The pistons swinging
up and down in a song
of exhaustion

II

She refuses to abide
by the engine's
deafening roar

Labour as it pleases,
have it feast on
her heat

Forming tracks
with bare bodies

at the expense of
blackened hands,
under-pressure
bruises

III

She rejects voicing
words that mould
her heart into
its faultless
shape

instead of yet more
tissue with valves
and an expiry date

A human with
desires and
uniqueness

RAT RACE

Doing, climbing, rat racing
Where is the silver lining?
Can you see it?

Blinds covering
splendid views,
nightfall pouring
over

Plunge into the cascades,
that sink deeper into mist
Erase the I and foresee
its past

Once back from the voyage,
the world will be a coin
flipped sideways—
both sides visible

MOLOTOV

I

After midnight,
I promised the
hallway to be
the perfect girl

To brush my teeth
twice a day,
to brush my hair
before bedtime

To brush the mess
under the carpet
and smile

What is there not
to be cheerful about?

Look at the world

Its unwearying
throb

The abundance
of goods

The full moon
casting light
on paved roads

We all fashion
our fortune,
isn't that
right?

Sometimes I have
the urge to shatter
No, to burn

To ignite
Molotov cocktails
and throw them
at the feet of
passers-by

Deface their mirages,
their well-built
bridges

Slap them
in the face
with fireballs,
stir them up
and shout

How their carefully
arranged lives
can go up
in smoke

and their pillars
can smash down
to ashes
(in seconds)

without an ear
to care

II

Curate the sadness'
wilted herbarium
above the vacant
fireplace—
a centrepiece,
don't hide it

Only then relief
will dawn from
the horizon

SNAKES AND LADDERS*

I

No one suspected
how many times
she had to start
from square one

And if she shared,
they did not listen
la la la la la

* "Snakes and Ladders" (also known as "Chutes and Ladders") is a classic board game for two players. The aim of the game is to reach the end of the board first. Squares with snakes bring you back and whereas stairs move you forward.

II

She gathered
boards and rungs
from around the world

Fashioned them
into ladders
inside her stomach

Her life was remodelled
into a game of
"Snakes and Ladders"

III

The play
commenced

She moved up,
sometimes down,
always diagonal

For most of the journey,
there was a teddy bear
next to her collarbone

and a handful of friends,
or people, rather,
that she knew

They talked
to her,
at her,
to themselves

about their holidays,
escapades,
sore hearts
(then cats and dogs)

filling the space
with others' stories
but
their interpretations,
their snakes
Down we slither

IV

Some people—
caught between steps,
others still hanging
                    onto
                        the
                        sides
                        of
                        ladders

Some people
fell from
the ladders

Some unleashed
snakes
and had her go back
a few squares
not once or twice

Others brought
ladders
and
helped
her
climb

WHAT ARE YOU AFRAID OF?

She asked at the dinner table

I replied, myself

Sometimes,
when I close
my eyes

and the past
starts dancing
over the screen
of the eyelids

The shadow
puppets emerge:

that conversation
with my boss
from nearly
three years ago,

five most awkward
encounters
with at the time
intense crushes

This morning—
running into
the delivery person
on the stairs

(How you should have
said it differently,
the shadows dancing,
feathers decorating
their shaven heads)

I'd rather delay
the world
with an hour

Let me watch some
YouTube Shorts,
let me listen
to some 2000s
throwback hits

Let me close
the curtains

the outside laughters
do not resonate,
the outside laughters,
the outside

SHE CHOSE
TO **HEAL**

I ADMIT, I AM AFRAID

Not to be afraid,
but to be still

To resonate only
with a heartbeat

For the world
to be convulsing
in its rhythm
around me
(without me)

Can I sprint
forward
while patching
from the past?

ADAPTATION WOUNDS

We all have fading scars
Weathered tectonic fissures,
resembling plain skin
to untrained eyes

Scars we don't allow to
define our contours

Despite their reminders
that they are at the core of
our geological relief

Wounds still open up—
sores that need salve
to smooth out,
to silken

Wounds to apply
ointment to,
daily

to fight off
the rising
pains

The ones we cuddle,
plow, turn inside out,
and water
to aid their revival
into a fertile soil

More fertile than
it was ever before

How is your
heart today?

(She asked,
staring at me)

Is it faint? Does it carry
its weight well?

Does it flutter, palpitate
when it's not
supposed to?

Do you hear its tiny eruptions,
fountains of blood and aches?

How many times
did it hold off
from imploding?

How many times
did it patch itself with
a needle and yarn?

How is your heart today?

(At first, her question
was alarming)

How could my heart
possibly be,
I murmured

I listened for a beat
in the chest

Nothing there

On the wrist—
index and middle finger
found a beat,
caught a rabbit
skin deep

(A sense of relief rushed through)

It is doing well, I replied

I am stretching it out,
stuffing lining, sewing
bat wings on its casing

Then it takes care
of itself
(mostly)

UNTITLED 2

When you tinker
with a splintered heart
and repair its aortas—

a mechanism
of a vintage clock

tick tock,
click

Tweeze out the chip
with bare hands

and push plasticine
down its throat to
fill up the gaps

Pour over it
buckets of care
(universal balm for hearts)

and brush the rust off,
oiling parts up
to smoothness

The mechanism
will then begin
its song

and all will fall
in place

THIS CREEK
IS A LIFESPRING

The flow of life heals
the rough patches

Hang in there,
my soul

HEAVIEST ROCK
TO LIFT

She chose
  to prioritise
    bandaging her feet,
      unbending the soul

Breaking
        the habit
of making excuses
        for others

Lifting rocks when
they are the **heaviest**

Catapulting them
away from her
footpath

UNDER
THE BRIDGE

Let's rediscover
the braids of the river
under the bridge

I know a place by the creeks
where frogs veil themselves
in water lilies

and turn into princes
whenever they wish

Let's soak our feet in,
sweep away anxieties

Brush off what is over
and done

In this cleansing moment,
the pins and needles
you stuck in me,

water
under the bridge

COME ROUND

I sometimes end up at
the same cornerstone,
no matter how far
these legs propel me

Still carrying the first
backpack mom bought
(from a grocery store)

Changing, adapting,
occasionally
found

But that is alright,
the unbeaten track
behind has turned
into
a foot trail

DECK OF CARDS

It is not about
ironing out
the rough edges
until it's perfect,
untarnished,
brand new

Healing is how high you
rise above your past self

Above the cards
you were dealt
to start the
journey
with

LIFE LONG EDUCATION

I know I didn't have the courage

Heart and brain—
give me a break,
I didn't mean to

Don't feed me
regrets in an
   irregular   rhythm

(As far as we remember)
we are all here
for the first time
and learning
takes time

STARFISH LIMBS

When affairs
go sideways,
how do you detach
your lizard tail?

Scurry away and
then regrow

Or split into two:
a brand new starfish
emerging from
a cut off
limb?

I would cherish it
to learn the magic

SIDEWAYS

We are a sum of
our experiences

Colourful, confused,
trees growing
s
  i
   d
    e
     w
      a
       y
        s

Still carving a way up
and reaching
heights

SHADOW OF A SUMMIT

Trust me, you are not a leaf,
to be swung about by winds

Rain will grow foliage on
your shoulders, to keep you
safe
From the nearing storms
From the ever-changing
weather

Sun will nurture your cells
in the depths of the well,
in your womb

Walking on dry soil hardens
the feet, prepares for voyage
on grouchy grounds

You evolve as
the seasons r o t a t e
the wheel of life

From a water sponge,
from other people's
emotional sponge

to a perched, bare,
1000-years old tree

Wisdom soaked into
its sap, its crust

Allowing time to embalm
years onto your tree-trunk,
the core becomes
well sheltered,
protected

Unmoved, the height
of your being hangs
soaring

A titan with a shadow
tall as a summit,
strong as a gale

SPOON-SHAPED

I gave myself all
is ever required:

tranquility
in the spine,

lightness
in the neck,

a space to fill
with love

here—
where desire lives
into a spoon-shape
under the spleen

ARCHIMEDES

Do not ask me why
I seem so downhearted,
in low spirits

I will not be able to
box it all inside,
within my body's
borders

I will not be able to
hold up the outpouring
of tears

They will break through
and spill out of my hands
out of my eyes,
chest and head,

Flooding the space
around and between

Only then I can lighten up,
an Archimedes principle[†]

Buoyancy pushing me up
to stay afloat and stabilise

[†] any body completely or partially submerged in a fluid at rest is
influenced by a buoyant force, the magnitude of which is equal to
the weight of the displaced fluid

FLOAT

The rising
pressure
from
inside

I recognise that
old feeling,
welcoming it
to the world

No longer afraid
of being afraid
I open my arms
and let it be

Plunging into
the bitter waters,
the fear subsides

Now floating
is easier
to the body

Rising—
softer
to the mind

OLD CHAPTER, NEW TALE

Levitating above the earth

Noticing the fields that
used to cuff me
to the ground

How ridiculous they look,
how limited and hairless

How the point of view
has changed the tale

and the dragons
are no longer
fire-breathing

How all seems so small
and the love for myself
keeps me lifting

SHE CHOSE
TO **BE**

CONSTRUCT A PLACE

Not knowing where the sidewalk
begins / where it terminates /
lift up one foot / then the other /
abstaining from predicting

Construct a place / catch a breath / as it
is conceived / create space / inside you
to inflate / pushing the outer shell /
ballooning

Until combustion / bursts the spirit /
into flames / thrusts you forward /
wheezing / gasping / with working fluid
made of soul-searching /
vulnerability / aspirations /
hopeful glaze

You are your own engine /
wondrous / briefly ignited /
hands on steering wheel /
heading into the future

EDGE OF THE BLANKET

I snatch the last summer days /
sniffing them in / at first, adagio / then
inhaling / as much as / lungs can
embrace / addict in a sunlight / attire

Nostrils shudder / goosebumps
over the lower half of the arms /
the air propels my feet to gallop /
to speed / towards the seashore

Towards the sun's glimmers /
slithering timelessness / going around
possibilities / grabbing /
the multitude of happenings / weaving
the freedom / reality

Leaving dents in the summer /
that will be there / for future
generations / to write poems
about / and search to sew
the threads together

Then / exhausted to bits /
satisfied to lunatism / feet
fall asleep / poking out /
the edge of the blanket

SUMMER'S ASCENDING

Your heart knows
you are not being
faithful to yourself

I open my arms and
welcome the sun rising
beneath my eyelids

Heart waves

I have grown to listen
to the waves of my
heart

Not to the ripples
others push through
open waters

The tide is high,
the spring inside
is plentiful

TESTAMENT

When the hands are weary

Their veins thickened by
the everyday
undertows

I walk to the moss-pressed hill
so far away
it has no human-given name
or guiding signs

and sigh

The top is sweeping up its mists,
clearing curtain of a view
unravelling itself—

a faithful dawn of
treetops and
crowns

A moment of solitude,
contemplating
the all in one

Nothing in this world
was promised
to me

and I am here
just breathing

NECK DEEP

I

I am neck deep in life and
its little shenanigans

Its crusty winter mornings
and the voids left
from goodbyes

Its random acts of kindness
and insufferable
selfishness

II

I am neck deep in sadness
the children's songs bring
through the rotting
windows

The punctual reminders
we will be dust and yet
we are bigger than
the sum of our
molecules

I am neck deep in joy
when the clock strikes
a New Year's midnight and
I have survived the annual
dull thump and sharp turns

III

When the seasons carry rebirth
and all I want for Christmas is
the world to be stopped by
a couple of loving hands

I am neck deep in
my own faults
and greatness

Shooting star
burning through
life,

sometimes with a bang,
sometimes wizzing away,
a candle in the wind

me

Multi, multi-faceted,
multi-faced

Cocoon unravelling
a butterfly

Story to be yet narrated,
story to be yet untold

Travelling through time,
growing, falling,
raising

Two feet firmly
on ground,
two cheeks up
in heavens

90% star leftovers,

90% fermented hopes,

90% me, a metamorphosis

All I ever needed

All I ever had

SAIL UPWARDS

The temporary grows
into eternal

Don't stay if you'd rather run

If there is a lump inside pushing
to spread into fireworks—
liberate

The roads wane
underneath the soles
until their pores are fractured
larks, the singing intensifies
as you move away

Worlds dying,
worlds blooming

Time's sands pouring
into tree-trunk rings

Time's sands passing
through your skin,
wrinkling its relief

Put the sails up,
prepare for winds,
correct the heeling,
take the helm
in your grip

Don't stay if you'd rather run

Set a course, weigh anchor
and cruise away

HANDS OF AUTUMN

I am living
strangers'
lives

Sliding down canals,
sprinting on the panels
of rooftops

Pouring into shafts,
cutting oval paths
through the mist

Slipping into abandoned
shoes and wearing them out
until they crumble
to pieces

I am hiding behind
the corners of eyes

Poking out from
the pocket of
your shirt

Flying in the air in
riding seeds of
a dandelion

Embracing you
tightly
from afar

through
the hands of the
coming autumn

EMBERS

The years have
consumed my eyes

The mirrors faded
from inspections

Now I can see lucid clear

Moving on is the holy water

With feet—dry twigs cold—
every footstep on Earth is
a dance challenge over
anastenarian[†] embers

[†] a traditional in some parts of Bulgaria and Greece
barefoot fire-walking and ecstatic dancing ritual

But, love,
it feels so right
to keep
walking

BE THE SILENCE

In a world spilling out
so much noise,
let me be the silence

The branches of the birch,
letting go of its leaves
without announcing

Let me bear the quiet love,
weaving straws and grass,
keeping the birds warm

Lets turn into a supernova
without an ear to hear it,
without a breath to gasp

A PEARL IN A BLACK SEA

Crescent moon,
you don't have
to be full

Just stay with me
and shed a light
on the path
forward

SHE CHOSE
TO **LOVE**

BUOYANCY

The sea cleanses
the city's rat race
from my pores

Washes away
the anxiety
of wanting
more

Reminds me I am
not here to stay

and being in love
with the pulse
is all

TOWARDS

Your chest cavity is a raft
after a shipwreck / set adrift
to move us / through seas /
riding unwrinkled / waves /
all the way / to the
underscore / of the horizon

Which was gone / and
now you brought it / back /
stitched it to land
and waters / the horizon /
which tumbles / where
the promised
land / stretches

The land / the flora and fauna /
painting together / pools of water /
hearts deep / liberation

There / my feet land into /
the heavy footsteps of yours /
stick into their shapes / glue-like /
there / the ocean of freedom / filled
to the brim / there / us / towards
the same direction

STARGAZINGS

Don't show me the stars—
step in and build a bridge
to their luminous bodies

So we can embark on
a voyage to the vast,
to infinities of mind
and body

Sculpt a new earth,
plant our feet into
the ground, so we
bloom

into what we are
meant to be to
relinquish our
inhibitions

Don't show me the stars—
here is where our home lies

In this green mess of a planet

Build the necessary on earth
to create a cozy space for us
where we can thrive
and relish

Where I have chosen to love
and nurture the life we create

Its jumble of colours
Its infinite striving

COSMIC AVOCADO ☉

Then my heart went cosmic

It prodded the thorax,
expanding with every gulp
rhonchi
      crackles
           wheeze

The ribs hollowed hum
broken through

Swelling and rounding,
an avocado core

Pushing out of its skin,
shedding its
cloak

Didn't consider
            slowing
                    down
until cities grew
miniature
in its curious belly

Now of a planetary
scale

Heartbeats spilling
            out of the earth
                        in waves

Breathing heart that
is searching
for you

Seeking to encompass
you and all the people
it loves
into its beats

It forms a ring
around the planet
to ensure

it can love you,
it can love itself,
it can love all
with every thump

Without searching
any further

PRISM-HEART

Catapulting
through
rains of love

Leave a trace—
a rainbow arc

Drops of freedom
tingle the cheeks
and remind us

not all showers
are evidence
of drowning

Our prism-hearts
disperse light

Babel

Life—a flash of light,
a tower of hide and seek,
a blink of an eye

On top of the walls—
multitude of tongue,
multitude of people

In its Hanging Gardens
don't plant anything
but love

CLOCK

I stop the minute
hand, the hour hand
halting to a pop

Another hour to kill

The clock freezes
and disintegrates
into crushed ice

The time is you

HUMAN CONDITION

Everyday we fall
for someone new

The way they touch
the handle of the tea
mug before raising it
up
and slurping

Their gestures—
at the same time
showy and shy

in a bouquet of
familiar mystery

Those lovers of light—
air clouding them

Their multitude of
arrivals and departures,
take-offs and landings

governed by
self-guided,
self-timed
schedules

Unlatching new
doors
as they leave

Untangling
heartstrings
as they come
back
round

Us wanting to
disappear in
them

Their bodies soft
as a welcome,
their hands
cold
as a coin

Every day we
choose to love

an angle of someone's
face
its waning moon
in a rod of light-play

our own silhouette
cocooned in
self-kindness

Laying sideways,
staring at
the new in us
and embracing

Excitement punctures
the veil of the everyday

Humans
are meant
to be adored

The rest is a play
of shadows on
a dressing
screen

FLAME

I will not ask you
where you
came from

Nor I will ask you
how many sunsets
did you hide
under the fold
of your collar

The past has already
drawn inky circles
around my eyes
and the mind
is weary

The spirits are high up
and the night is pagan

We sit here surrounded
by flickering lights

The bodies dancing
in a rapture of flames

The sun-flares
out of my heart
grow longer

It seems we are
diving together
in blaze

I will not ask you
where you
came from

Just tell me
where together
we'll head

DEWDROPS

The
dews
over
your
pure
soul,
mini
universe

The
gleam
over
your
petal
eyes, I
am love
struck

T h e

c l o u d s

o v e r

y o u r

p u r e

soul, let

m   e

swallow

them

SHE CHOSE TO LOVE

She chose love

Not the type
that sticks you
to people

and you cannot
get yourself
untangled,
unglued

Not the type
to leave you
thirsty and
longing,
dragging your feet
and confused

She chose love
that made her
light

That acknowledged
how short life is

How happenings
have an end
and how
we can rediscover
awe and
adoration

in ourselves
and the world
every day
as we breathe
bit by bit

And not search in
someone else's
eyes
for the love
we haven't given
ourselves

ACKNOWLEDGEMENTS

Women often appear in my poetry with their inner strength and innate ability to love and empower. They emerge in it with their life creating capacity and limitless strength of spirit.

This is because of the enormous influence two women have on my life—my mother and my grandmother.

I have learned all I know from them. Not about the world of science or literature. But about being a human and an artist. They have taught me how to be both vulnerable and resilient, how to communicate with the innermost parts of myself without fear.

They have planted the seeds of love in me, packed wisdom for me to thrive on. They helped me carry myself through heartbreak, rejection, disappointment, hurt, to name a few.

Without their nourishing hands and words, my journey would have been different, perhaps rougher.

Without the enormous strength of our mothers, grandmothers and great-grandmothers, we wouldn't be who we are today.

Without the strength of generations of humans and their robustness to continue onwards, we wouldn't be here, facing yet another day with what we can.

I dedicate this book to all of us— for resisting the voices of the outside, the inner and outer critics, and finding the courage to be ourselves and fight on.

For getting up when we feel we should give up, for trying again and again to live our best lives in the face of change and uncertainty.

Moreover, I can't pass on the opportunity to also dedicate some of these poems to the ones that left us with hurt.

Their lessons have made us learn. They have unravelled a well of power within us and have made us grow.

I would also like to dedicate the love inside this book to my caring partner.

The one that has showed me parts of myself I didn't know I had. The one that has been beside me in my toughest moments.

Love is only a word until you experience it.

LOVE,
Yvette

About the Author

Yvette Dulo is a writer and a believer in the healing power of words and inner exploration.

She loves loving, loves creating and building a space in the world through poetry where empowerment can thrive.

The meaning behind human circumstances and their influence on a person's life have always driven her creative pursuits.

In her work, she strives to be painfully honest, impactful and self-confessional, at the same time speaking with the voices of many.

Thus, showcasing the transformation we are all capable of through narratives of hope and self-reliance.

When she asked her friends to describe her with a couple of words, they all struggled.

Then poured out a multitude of adjectives such as radiating, natural force, kind, imperfect, human.

"She chose to love" is just the beginning.

Dear reader,

Thank you for spending time with
"She chose to love"!

I truly appreciate you being here.

If you enjoyed this book, please consider leaving
a review on Amazon or Goodreads.

It really helps the efforts of independent artists.

Thank you!

Published by
Yvette Dulo Publishing

Printed in Great Britain
by Amazon

42053599R00076